Original title:
With Every Scar

Copyright © 2024 Swan Charm
All rights reserved.

Author: Daisy Dewi
ISBN HARDBACK: 978-9916-79-221-6
ISBN PAPERBACK: 978-9916-79-222-3
ISBN EBOOK: 978-9916-79-223-0

The Spirit's Paradox of Pain

In shadows deep, where whispers dwell,
The spirit bends, yet does not break.
Through trials fierce, the heart can swell,
In pain's embrace, we find our wake.

A paradox, this road we tread,
With every thorn, the bloom appears.
In sorrow's grip, our truths are fed,
A tapestry woven in our tears.

So lift your gaze to skies above,
Beyond the strife, a light remains.
In every hurt, a thread of love,
Through sacred wounds, our spirit gains.

Harvest the strength from every fall,
Within each ache, a lesson found.
The spirit's song will gently call,
In pain, the soul is truly crowned.

Let grief be not a weight we bear,
But wings upon which we will rise.
In paradox, we learn to care,
With faith igniting our goodbyes.

Embracing the Shards of Life

Each shard of life, a crystal bright,
Reflecting both the joy and strife.
In brokenness, we find our sight,
Embracing shards, we shape our life.

For every wound that cuts so deep,
A story waits to see the day.
Within the pain, the heart will leap,
And from those shards, we'll find our way.

The beauty lies in fractured hearts,
In imperfections, love will glow.
Each piece a canvas that imparts,
The art of living, high and low.

When darkness creeps and shadows loom,
We gather light from every crack.
With every shard, we find our bloom,
In unity, no turning back.

So let us stand with arms outspread,
In acceptance, grace begins to flow.
Embracing shards, by love we're led,
In every breath, our spirits grow.

Illuminating the Darkest Corners

In darkest nights, when hope feels lost,
The flicker faint, yet fiercely burns.
With every step, we count the cost,
Illuminating, the heart returns.

A candle's light in shadows cast,
Reminds us we are not alone.
Each flicker breaks the heavy past,
In darkness, we have softly grown.

So lift your lamps to chase the dread,
In corners where despair can creep.
With whispered prayers, we forge ahead,
Illuminating the paths we keep.

Through trials deep, a beacon shines,
A guiding star to hold us near.
In darkest corners, love defines,
The strength we find through every tear.

Let faith be light to guide your way,
As dawn breaks free from night's tight hold.
In every moment, seek the day,
Illuminating courage bold.

Sacred Soil of Suffering

In sacred soil, our roots go deep,
From every tear, the earth will grow.
Through suffering, the heart will weep,
Yet from this pain, new seeds bestow.

With every storm, we bend and sway,
Yet find the strength to rise anew.
The soil's embrace brings forth the day,
In suffering, the soul breaks through.

Within the ache, the promise waits,
For every trial, the growth will show.
The harvest blooms, as love creates,
In sacred soil, our spirits glow.

Let roots entwine in tender grace,
With every wound, a lesson learned.
In suffering's depths, we find our place,
A fertile ground where hope is earned.

So bless the pain, embrace the hurt,
For from the grief, the flowers speak.
In sacred soil, our spirits flirt,
With life's great beauty, bold and meek.

Adorned with Adversity

In trials we are forged anew,
With every tear, our faith grew.
The weight of burdens, yet we stand,
In grace and strength, we hold Your hand.

Through darkest nights, Your light shines bright,
In storms of doubt, You're our delight.
Each hardship, Lord, a chance to see,
The beauty in this tapestry.

When shadows creep and hope feels fleet,
We find Your whispers, soft and sweet.
In anguish, love begins to birth,
A journey from despair to worth.

So clad in trials, we wear our scars,
Reminders of Your guiding stars.
With every step, we rise and soar,
Adorned with faith, forevermore.

Pearls of Wisdom from Sorrow

In moments heavy, wisdom grows,
In silent tears, the spirit knows.
Each sorrow holds a pearl divine,
A glimpse of grace, a sacred sign.

From brokenness, our hearts are made,
In shadows deep, our fears cascade.
Yet through the pain, we learn to feel,
The strength of faith, a sacred seal.

The night may seem to stretch for days,
But dawn will break in joyful rays.
Through trials, love begins to mold,
The heart prepared to find pure gold.

Each lesson carved in silent strife,
A map that guides us through this life.
In every tear, a truth unfurls,
Selah—embrace the hidden pearls.

The Sanctuary of Shadows

In whispers soft, the shadows dwell,
A sacred place where spirits swell.
In solitude, we find the grace,
To seek the light in hidden space.

The quiet heart, it learns to see,
The beauty in simplicity.
In darkened rooms where fears abide,
We find a Savior by our side.

With open arms, He beckons near,
In shadow's clutch, we shed our fear.
The sanctuary, a hallowed ground,
Where peace and love can still be found.

Through trials faced in silent night,
We cultivate a deeper sight.
For in the dark, we learn to grow,
The seeds of faith, like rivers flow.

Narratives of the Nailed

In stories told of sacrifice,
We find redemption, so precise.
The nails that bind, they do not break,
For love endured for our own sake.

From scars of pain, a tale unfolds,
In every wound, the heart upholds.
A journey marked with trial and grace,
In every step, we seek Your face.

The cross of burdens, heavy sighs,
Yet through the ache, the spirit flies.
In narratives of those who tread,
The path of love, where hope is shed.

Each chapter written in the soul,
An echo of the greater whole.
In stories shared, our hearts arise,
United by Your sacrifice.

The Hymn of the Healer's Path

In the light of grace we tread,
With whispers soft, where angels lead,
Each step a prayer, the heart is fed,
In healing's arms, we are freed.

Through valleys deep, where shadows crawl,
We raise our song, a sweet refrain,
For every wound and every fall,
The Healer's touch brings peace from pain.

The rivers flow with solace pure,
A balm for souls, a guiding hand,
With faith unbound, our hearts endure,
Together on this sacred land.

With every note a spirit soars,
In unity, we seek to rise,
For love awakens, never wars,
A beacon bright 'neath endless skies.

As dawn unfolds, a promise shines,
In the light of love, we find our way,
Forever linked, our spirit twines,
The Healer's path, the light of day.

The Silence of the Scarred

In quietude, the heart does mend,
Beneath the weight of trials past,
A soft embrace, where sorrows bend,
In silence found, we breathe at last.

The scars we wear, a tale unspun,
Each line a mark, a journey drawn,
Yet in the night, hope's whisper won,
Beneath the stars, we greet the dawn.

For every tear that left a trace,
In solitude, strength starts to bloom,
Within the silence, we find grace,
A sacred space where fears consume.

With gentle hands, the spirit cleans,
The echoes fade, they gently part,
In every wound, the light redeems,
The silence speaks to every heart.

Awake, we rise to greet the fight,
For every scar has led us far,
In healing light, we find our sight,
Embracing all, we shine like stars.

Dancing with Deliverance

With joyful hearts, we take the stage,
In rhythm sweet, our spirits soar,
With every step, we turn the page,
Deliverance blooms, forevermore.

In sacred circles, we move as one,
With laughter bright, we break the chains,
Each twirl a prayer, the battle won,
As faith ignites, we shed our pains.

To music soft, our souls entwine,
In harmony, our hopes align,
The dance of life, a grand design,
With every beat, we feel divine.

The light surrounds, a warm embrace,
In every sway, we find our peace,
With open hearts, we seek His face,
In dancing joy, our souls release.

As twilight falls, we lift our song,
Together strong, we never part,
For in this dance, we all belong,
Deliverance whispers in the heart.

In the Shadow of the Healer

In the shadow, our fears reside,
Yet softly there, His light will shine,
With gentle hands, He'll be our guide,
In healing's grace, our hearts align.

When burdens weigh and spirits break,
With every breath, we lean on hope,
In whispered prayers, our souls awake,
The healer's touch, a sacred scope.

Through trials faced and battles waged,
In darkest nights, His light appears,
With every wound, our faith engaged,
In trust, we shed our silent tears.

The journey long, with steps unsure,
Yet in His presence, we find strength,
For every scar, a path made pure,
In love's embrace, we go the length.

With every heartbeat, we rise anew,
In shadows cast, His grace will gleam,
For in the healer, we find the true,
A promise held within the dream.

Mending the Spirit's Fabric

In the silence, whispers grow,
Threads of hope begin to sew.
Hearts once torn, now gently bind,
In love's embrace, true peace we find.

Faith, a needle piercing through,
Stitching wounds, both old and new.
Under skies of azure grace,
We seek the light, a warm embrace.

Tears may fall like drops of rain,
Every tear, a thread of pain.
Yet in sorrow, beauty's stitched,
From brokenness, our souls are rich.

Hands uplifted, we shall mend,
In divine love, we transcend.
With every knot, a story told,
Hearts renewed, like threads of gold.

Graceful Remnants

In shadows cast by yesterday,
Lie remnants of a brighter day.
Echoes soft, like whispered cheer,
Guide the way, the path is clear.

Scars adorn the heart with grace,
Each one tells a sacred place.
In imperfections, beauty shines,
A tapestry that love designs.

Life's old chains now gently break,
In every falter, strength we make.
From ash and dust, we rise anew,
In grace, we find our spirit true.

Hold the remnants, cherish all,
For in each stumble, we stand tall.
A gentle hand, a heart so wide,
In every flaw, love's truth will guide.

The Prayer of the Imperfect

Awake, O heart, from earthly plight,
In prayer's soft glow, embrace the light.
Imperfect souls, we gather near,
With whispered hopes, and dreams sincere.

Beneath the weight of endless doubt,
We seek the truth; we long to shout.
Though darkness lingers in our minds,
In unity, a peace we find.

Gather our flaws, they make us whole,
Each crack reveals a story's role.
In every flaw, a prayer's grace,
With every breath, He knows our pace.

So raise your voice, let tears flow free,
In this communion, we shall see.
For in our struggles, spirit grows,
Imperfect hearts, to Him, we pose.

Celestial Tapestry

Stars above weave tales of old,
Threads of silver, stories bold.
In the night, a sacred dance,
A cosmic script of chance and chance.

Galaxies spin in quiet grace,
Each swirl a truth we long to trace.
In this vastness, find our place,
An endless love, a warm embrace.

The fabric of our lives is spun,
In every battle, we have won.
In every heart, a light so bright,
Guiding souls through darkest night.

With heavenly hands, we craft our fate,
In unity, we celebrate.
A tapestry of love and faith,
Each thread a promise, life's true wraith.

The Holy Ledger of Hurt

In sacred ink, our sorrows write,
Each tear a verse of muted light,
The ledger holds our pain and grace,
A testament to our embrace.

In shadows deep, we find our way,
Through trials faced, we learn to pray,
Each wound a page, each scar a sign,
A holy tale of love divine.

The burdens carried, etched in flesh,
Transforming sorrow, truth enmesh,
In every hurt, a whisper loud,
Of hope that rises, unbowed.

We gather burdens, lift them high,
To heaven's throne we aim our cry,
In every heartbreak, faith ignites,
The ledger glows with inner lights.

So let the pages turn with grace,
Where hurt and hope find their place,
In holy ledger, we draw near,
Embracing love, dispelling fear.

Spiritual Whispers in the Wounds

In every wound, a whisper flows,
A lesson wrapped in silent throes,
The spirit speaks through aching flesh,
In deep despair, our souls refresh.

Each scar a story, each tear a prayer,
For healing grace is always there,
The whispers guide through darkened nights,
Transforming pain to sacred sights.

Within the hurt, a light resides,
A flame of hope where love abides,
In every struggle, strength we find,
Spiritual whispers intertwine.

We journey forth, through trials grim,
With faith as anchor, never dim,
The wounds of life, a sacred art,
Each whisper nourishes the heart.

So tend the wounds with tender care,
In every breath, let spirits wear,
The fabric of our shared design,
Where whispers heal, and souls align.

When the Heart Breaks Open

When hearts do break, the light pours in,
An open door where love begins,
In shattered pieces, beauty shines,
A canvas vast of holy lines.

Each crack a pathway to the grace,
That nurtures wounds with soft embrace,
In brokenness, the spirit sings,
A melody of fragile things.

With every heartbeat, hope takes flight,
Through darkest hours, we find the light,
In vulnerability, strength is seen,
When hearts break open, souls convene.

The journey soft, yet filled with fire,
In every fall, we rise, aspire,
For in the depths, redemption grows,
Through heart's embrace, true love bestows.

So let us gather, love unveiled,
In every tear, the heart is hailed,
When brokenness reveals the way,
Transformation blooms, in light's array.

Holiness etches on Flesh

Holiness carved where pain resides,
In every scar, the spirit guides,
The body bears the marks of grace,
Each line a map, our sacred place.

Through trials faced, a deeper trust,
In ashes, hope will rise from dust,
In tender flesh, divinity stays,
As holiness etches loving ways.

The wounds we bear become our song,
A harmony that makes us strong,
In every heartbeat, faith's embrace,
Anointing us with sacred space.

With open arms, we carry on,
Transforming hurt to love reborn,
In holiness, the truth is found,
Our lives a prayer, profound, unbound.

So let us honor every mark,
For in the shadows, shines a spark,
Holiness etched deep within,
A journey blessed where life begins.

Songs from the Depths of Sorrow

In shadows deep, where silence reigns,
Whispers of hope break these chains.
A heart once full, now worn and torn,
Yet in the night, a light is born.

With every tear, a prayer ascends,
To heavens high, where mercy lends.
The soul finds strength in trials faced,
In darkest hours, grace is embraced.

Amidst the pain, a dawn shall rise,
Transforming tears into joyous cries.
For every loss, a lesson learned,
Through fire's heat, the spirit yearned.

O weary path, lead me to peace,
From sorrow's grip, let my fears cease.
In faith I stand, though storms I face,
For in His love, I find my place.

Lift up the soul, with hymns of light,
In darkest valleys, He is my might.
With grateful heart, I'll sing His praise,
For in His arms, my spirit stays.

The Graceful Odyssey

In the silence of the dawn, I seek,
Whispers of the Divine, soft and meek.
Guided by the stars, I tread the way,
Each step a prayer, leading me to stay.

Through valleys low and mountains high,
With faith as my compass, I reach for the sky.
The journey unfolds, a tapestry grand,
Woven with love by the Creator's hand.

In trials I find my spirit's test,
In shadows of doubt, I find my rest.
A heart transformed by grace's embrace,
Each wound a lesson, each scar a trace.

With every moment, I learn to be still,
In the depths of my soul, I find the will.
To tread the unknown with courage anew,
For I walk this path, guided by You.

As I reach the horizon, where waters flow,
I offer my thanks for blessings that grow.
In this graceful odyssey, I find my peace,
In the love of the Beloved, my soul's release.

Celestial Marks of the Beloved

In the night sky, Your light shines bright,
Celestial marks that guide me right.
Each star a promise, a bond divine,
In the vast unknown, Your love does shine.

With each heartbeat, I feel Your grace,
In every moment, I seek Your face.
The moon whispers secrets, ancient and bold,
Tales of redemption, forever retold.

In the breath of the wind, I hear Your song,
A melody pure, where I belong.
Through mountains and rivers, the voices call,
In their sacred echo, I feel it all.

Your love is the anchor in troubled seas,
In Your gentle presence, my spirit finds ease.
I gather the stars, like pearls at dawn,
Each one a token of the love I lean on.

Oh Beloved, my heart's deepest delight,
In Your embrace, I find my flight.
Celestial marks lead my wandering soul,
In the tapestry of love, I am made whole.

The Armor of Experience

In life's fierce battle, I wear my shield,
Forged by the fire, my wounds revealed.
Each scar a story, a lesson learned,
In the light of wisdom, my spirit yearned.

With armor strengthened by trials faced,
I stand unwavering, by grace embraced.
The weight of the world may burden the soul,
Yet faith is the strength that makes me whole.

In shadows that linger, I find the light,
A beacon of hope in the darkest night.
With courage as my sword, I face the storm,
In the warmth of belief, I am reborn.

Every challenge, a step in the fight,
A dance with the day, a prayer at night.
With each breath I take, I learn to trust,
In the armor of experience, I rise from dust.

And though the path may twist and bend,
I march with grace, until the end.
For in every struggle, God's love draws near,
The armor of experience calms every fear.

Healing Water from the Well

In the depths of my heart, a wellspring flows,
Healing water that mends and knows.
Each drop a blessing, a soothing balm,
In the storm's fury, it whispers calm.

When the world feels heavy, I come to drink,
In the quiet moments, I pause and think.
The essence of life, pure and profound,
In every sip, Your love I've found.

From pain's dark corners, I draw the light,
Each wave a promise, glowing bright.
In the embrace of Your grace, I'm renewed,
Healing water flows, restoring my mood.

As I share this gift, a sacred trust,
In the hearts of others, I plant the dust.
The well never falters, its depths divine,
In community's arms, the threads intertwine.

So let us gather round this healing stream,
In faith and love, we work as a team.
For the water from the well is a gift to share,
A testament of hope in life's tender care.

The Sacred Journey of Suffering

In the valley of shadows, we tread,
With hearts heavy, seeking the thread.
Through trials fierce, we find our way,
In pain's embrace, we learn to pray.

Each tear a testament, each sigh a plea,
A path of suffering, yet we see.
The light within, a flicker's glow,
Guiding us gently, where we must go.

Broken and bruised, yet hope remains,
As love surrounds, and spirit gains.
For every cross that we must bear,
A purpose unfolds—He is there.

From ashes rise, with courage bold,
A story of faith, in silence told.
With every burden, grace will bloom,
Transforming our darkness to light's warm room.

So let the journey carve its mark,
In every sorrow, ignites the spark.
For through our suffering, we belong,
In sacred unity, we grow strong.

Blessings in Brokenness

In shattered pieces, beauty lies,
A heart once whole, now learns to rise.
In every crack, a light shines through,
A tender mercy, ever true.

Through trials that seem too great to bear,
The hand of grace is always near.
In brokenness, we find the way,
To blessings hidden, brightening our day.

Every stumble, every fall,
Leads to the one who hears our call.
For in our weakness, strength is found,
A sacred circle, love unbound.

The spirit mends what life has torn,
From grief and sorrow, we are reborn.
In every heartbeat, whispers loud,
Renouncing fear, we stand unbowed.

So let us cherish every scar,
A testament to how we are.
In blessings forged through trials faced,
Together we walk, forever graced.

Spiritual Imprints

In quiet moments, souls align,
With every breath, the stars entwine.
Awakened hearts, like rivers flow,
In spiritual imprints, love will grow.

Through whispers soft, the spirit speaks,
In silence deep, it gently peaks.
A hint of grace in every thought,
In every lesson, wisdom taught.

Beneath the surface, ripples spread,
In sacred spaces where we've tread.
Each encounter, a sacred thread,
In the tapestry of life, we're led.

Through trials faced, through joy and pain,
In every loss, something to gain.
The imprints linger, shaping our soul,
In every struggle, we become whole.

So let the journey carve its sign,
In every heartbeat, love, divine.
For spiritual imprints guide our way,
With every dawn, a brand new day.

Resilience of the Soul

Through storms we rise, through winds we bend,
With every challenge, we ascend.
In strength unseen, the spirit thrives,
Resilience blooms, where love survives.

In troubled waters, faith is found,
With every step, our hearts unbound.
Through fire's trial, we find our place,
In every moment, we embrace grace.

The journey bends, but never breaks,
In trembling hands, the spirit wakes.
For every tear that falls in strife,
A testament to the dance of life.

In unity, the weary stand,
Together bound by love's own hand.
Through darkest nights, we find the dawn,
In resilience, we've always drawn.

So let the soul's power illuminate,
With every heartbeat, let us create.
For in our struggles, hope does gleam,
A tapestry of life's grand dream.

A Testament Written in Tears

In shadows deep, where sorrows flow,
A heart laid bare, in pain we grow.
Each tear a prayer, a silent plea,
To find the light, to set us free.

In whispers soft, the Spirit speaks,
In darkest nights, our solace seeks.
The weight of grief, a heavy shroud,
Yet in it all, we stand unbowed.

For every loss, a lesson learned,
In every heart, a fire burned.
A testament of love profound,
In tears of hope, grace can be found.

The road is long, the path is steep,
Yet faith's embrace will never sleep.
From trials faced, we rise anew,
A sacred bond, our spirits true.

So let the tears fall, pure and clear,
They water seeds of love sincere.
With open hearts, we shall ascend,
In testament, our souls commend.

The Divine Dance of Healing

In the stillness of a whispered prayer,
The sacred breath, a gentle air.
A dance of grace, both soft and strong,
In every heartbeat, we belong.

When silence falls and shadows play,
The spirit stirs, the night turns day.
With every step, we find our way,
In love's embrace, we choose to stay.

Through trials faced, and wounds laid bare,
The dance of healing, a sacred care.
With open arms, we come alive,
In unity, our souls revive.

As rivers flow and candles flicker,
The light of hope grows ever quicker.
In every twirl, a story told,
Of faith unbroken and hearts made bold.

So let us join in this divine waltz,
A celebration of love's exalts.
With every turn, the spirits sing,
In the dance of life, we are the spring.

Echoes from the Depths

In the quiet void, where echoes dwell,
The whispers rise, tales hard to tell.
A journey deep, through valleys wide,
In faith we walk, and hope our guide.

Each heartbeat feels the sacred tune,
Beneath the stars, beneath the moon.
The echoes call from depths afar,
In darkest nights, we see the star.

The stories linger, the shadows glint,
In every pause, a heart beginning to hint.
From ancient times, their wisdom flows,
In every soul, the truth bestows.

Through trials faced and battles fought,
In silence held, the lessons taught.
We speak our truth, the world will hear,
In echoes from the depths, we steer.

So let the echoes guide our way,
In unity, we find our sway.
A chorus rises, a song of grace,
In echoes soft, we find our place.

Faith Forged in Fire

In flames that flicker, in shadows cast,
The furnace burns, the die is cast.
Through trials fierce, our spirits rise,
In faith's embrace, we touch the skies.

Each ember glows, a light divine,
With every breath, our souls entwine.
The heat of life, a test of might,
In darkest hours, we find the light.

The forge of love, where hearts ignite,
In every struggle, we find our right.
Strength from the fire, a bitter loss,
Yet through it all, we bear our cross.

With faith as armor, we'll brave the storm,
United together, our spirits warm.
Through trials faced, our hearts will soar,
In faith forged in fire, forevermore.

So let the flames dance, let the passion grow,
In the trial's heat, our strength will show.
With every spark, a purpose true,
In faith forged in fire, we rise anew.

Heaven's Tapestry of Trials

In shadows cast, the light breaks through,
Each tear a stitch, a path anew.
The trials shaped with love's embrace,
In heaven's loom, we find our place.

From thorns of pain, blooms rise high,
Whispers of hope in the sky.
Through storms we walk, hand in hand,
In faith's strong grip, forever stand.

The journey bends, but spirits rise,
With every fall, we reach the skies.
Faith guides us on, through darkest night,
In trials' fire, we find our light.

Grace threads the fabric, bright and bold,
In every heart, a story told.
United souls in love's great dance,
In heaven's plan, we find our chance.

So trust the tapestry we share,
In every moment, God is there.
Each trial faced, a sacred bond,
In heaven's arms, our spirits respond.

Marks of Grace Beneath the Skin

In every scar, a story lies,
A testament to love's sweet ties.
Each mark engraved, a whispered grace,
A map of trials we all face.

With gentle hands, the wounds we heal,
In sharing pain, our hearts reveal.
Life's canvas stained with all we've fought,
Through every battle, wisdom's sought.

Beneath the skin, a light so rare,
Forgiveness blooms in timeless care.
Each grace bestowed, a sacred gift,
In every heart, our spirits lift.

The marks we bear are not in vain,
For through the hurt, we find our gain.
In unity, our souls entwine,
With love's deep roots, our hearts align.

So let us wear our scars with pride,
For in them all, the truth can't hide.
Through trials faced, we find our song,
In every mark, we all belong.

Wounds of Wisdom

In every wound, there lies a door,
A passage through to something more.
The lessons learned, though often tough,
In grace we find our spirits rough.

With open hearts, we dare to feel,
The bitter truths that help us heal.
In silence deep, the whispers speak,
Through wounds of wisdom, we grow meek.

Each bruise a tale of strength and strife,
Crafting the patterns of our life.
In moments dark, the light will break,
From heavy hearts, new flares we make.

So let us cherish every scar,
As bright reminders of how far.
In wisdom's seat, we take our stand,
With open eyes, we seek His hand.

The wounds of wisdom carve the way,
To greater truths that guide our stay.
In every heart, a story swells,
Through trials faced, our spirit bells.

The Sacred Stories of Our Souls

In every heartbeat, a story spins,
A sacred dance where life begins.
The truths we hold in silence deep,
Are treasures we together keep.

With hands outstretched, we share our night,
In vulnerable moments, we find light.
Each life a tale, a vibrant hue,
In every soul, the love shines through.

The whispers soft, the echoes loud,
In joy and sorrow, we are proud.
Each journey shared, a sacred trust,
In hope's embrace, we all adjust.

In trials faced and victories won,
Our spirits soar, forever one.
In love's embrace, our stories blend,
In every heart, a faithful friend.

So let us gather, hand in hand,
In sacred spaces, together we stand.
With open hearts, let us all be,
A tapestry of unity.

Redemption on the Rough Path

In shadows deep, where we may stray,
The weary heart finds hope to stay.
With every step on stones so tough,
The soul finds grace, it is enough.

With faith as guide through trials wide,
In silence, hear the voice inside.
The road may bend, but not our will,
In every storm, Your love we feel.

Through thorns and pain, the spirits rise,
In darkest nights, we seek the skies.
Each tear we shed, a seed of light,
Blooms in the heart to shine so bright.

Upon the path of rocky tears,
In brokenness, Your love appears.
With every bruise, a story told,
Of mercy's hand, and grace unrolled.

The roughest trails may lead us home,
In tangled roots, we freely roam.
With open hearts and lifted eyes,
We find redemption, hope, and ties.

The Light Shines Through the Cracks.

In crevices where shadows fall,
A gentle glow begins to call.
Through broken walls, Your love breaks free,
It fills the void, it speaks to me.

Each blemish tells of battles fought,
In darkest hours, it is not naught.
The light, it filters in with grace,
Reflecting truth in every space.

Through every crack, a story beams,
Of hope restored and cherished dreams.
In fragile hearts, Your strength we find,
Illuminating all mankind.

Though life may bruise and wear us thin,
Your light within shines bright, within.
Each crack a canvas, bold and grand,
Where joy and sorrow walk hand in hand.

And so we rise, though parts may break,
With every flaw, a path we make.
In every light, our spirits sing,
Through cracks of life, Your love we bring.

Wounds of Grace

Oh wounds that ache, yet heal the soul,
In scars, we find a holy whole.
Each hurt a mark of grace divine,
In brokenness, Your light will shine.

Through trials faced, the heart grows strong,
In weakness found, we still belong.
For every tear, a lesson learned,
In every fire, the spirit burned.

The weight of pain brings forth the bloom,
In every shadow, grace finds room.
A tender heart, though marked with strife,
Transforms the wounds into new life.

To bear the scars is not in vain,
For from our struggles, love we gain.
In wounds of grace, the spirit thrives,
A testament of how love lives.

So lift your eyes and see the light,
For every wound, there comes the night.
Yet dawn will break, with hope ablaze,
In every heart, the wounds of grace.

Testament of the Bruised

In bruised and battered hearts we find,
The strength to rise, the truth refined.
Each mark a tale of struggles faced,
A testament of love embraced.

Through storms of doubt and waves of pain,
We journey on, though we may wane.
With every bruise, a story shared,
In unity, our souls are bared.

The trials faced, each tear we've shed,
A path to truth where angels tread.
For in the fray, our spirits soar,
The bruised will rise and seek for more.

In hearts that ache, compassion grows,
Each bruise a seed of love that sows.
For in the darkness, light will beam,
A testament of hope's sweet dream.

So let us walk with heads held high,
In every bruise, a reason why.
For through our strife, our truth is proved,
A testament of love, we move.

Healing Beyond the Hurt

From ashes rise the spirit bright,
In shadows fades the aching night.
With every tear, a river flows,
The heart unveils what mercy knows.

In faith we find a gentle hand,
A guiding light in sacred land.
Each wound a sign of love's embrace,
A journey carved through time and space.

Hope speaks softly in the breeze,
Whispers tend to weary knees.
Through trials, strength is softly found,
The soul restored, complete, unbound.

The healer walks beside each soul,
In silence makes the broken whole.
With every step, the path we tread,
Is steeped in grace and softly led.

So raise your eyes, release the pain,
In every loss, the love remains.
For healing flows from heart to heart,
A sacred weave, a work of art.

Chronicles of Triumph

In battles fierce, our spirits grow,
Through tempests wild, our faith we sow.
Each chapter penned in tears and dust,
Marks of our struggle, hope, and trust.

We rise as one, in unity true,
With every loss, our hearts renew.
A legacy forged in love and light,
For in the darkness, we seek what's right.

The whispers of the ancients hum,
In sacred spaces, victories come.
Through trials faced, the pages turn,
In every dusk, a dawn we yearn.

Hands lifted high, we sing aloud,
Of strength bestowed, we stand unbowed.
With every word, a story told,
Our spirits shine, resilient bold.

Join in the chorus, voices blend,
In triumph's name, our hearts ascend.
For through the strife, a path we carve,
In unity, we rise and starve.

Surviving Grace

In darkest hours, a light will gleam,
A whisper soft, a gentle dream.
With every breath, a chance we take,
In mercy's arms, we learn to wake.

Through thorny paths, our feet shall tread,
In sorrow's wake, we find our thread.
Each moment holds a sacred space,
In trials borne, we meet His grace.

When all seems lost, we hold the flame,
In every heart, He knows our name.
For in the void, His love will fill,
Embracing all, He bends our will.

With steadfast hope, we walk the line,
In brokenness, a soul divine.
And as the stars above will shine,
We find our peace in love's design.

So let us dance, through tears and strife,
In every wound, we find our life.
For grace, it flows like rivers wide,
In trusting hearts, our fears subside.

The Anointed Wounds

In quiet nights, where shadows play,
The wounds we bear will light the way.
Each scar a story, love's embrace,
Anointed paths we bravely trace.

Through hardships deep, our spirits soar,
In healing hearts, we find restore.
The echoes of our struggles sing,
A melody of grace they bring.

In every tear, a glimpse of gold,
A treasure found in stories told.
Each hurt becomes a sacred song,
In unity, where we belong.

The healer walks where pain will tread,
In humble hearts, His light is spread.
With every step, redemption blooms,
From brokenness, new life resumes.

So let the wounds be seen and known,
For in each mark, His love has grown.
We find our strength, our spirit's tune,
In every shadow, shines a boon.

Fragments of Faith

In the silence of the night,
whispers of hope ignite,
light pierces shadowed doubt,
faith finds its way out.

In the hearts of the weary,
love's ember shines clearly,
each fragment a sacred part,
binding us heart to heart.

Through trials fierce and long,
we gather strength in song,
every tear that we shed,
nourishes what we've said.

In the storm's raging face,
we seek the quiet grace,
with hands lifted high,
we let our spirits fly.

For in every broken piece,
God's promise brings us peace,
each step we courageously tread,
leads us closer to the thread.

The Marks of Mercy

With every scar that we bear,
  mercy's fingerprints are there,
    in the shadow of our pain,
hope blooms bright once again.

Through the trials we endure,
  love's gentle touch is sure,
    it mends what life has torn,
  in the light, we are reborn.

We find grace in every fall,
  His whispers echo the call,
redemption flows like the tide,
  washing over hearts wide.

In the depths of our sorrow,
  we glimpse a bright tomorrow,
  where every wound is healed,
    and love's truth is revealed.

So let us cherish the marks,
  the signs of love's bright sparks,
  for in mercy's warm embrace,
    we find our rightful place.

Hymn of the Healed

Awake, oh weary soul,
let the cries of joy console,
for every burden we've borne,
now be changed, transformed.

In the garden of His grace,
we find our rightful place,
healed in heart, renewed in mind,
with every step we find.

Voices raised in the air,
harmonies rich and rare,
singing songs of the free,
in Him, we find our glee.

Our wounds no longer bind,
in His light, we unwind,
scars tell stories we share,
of love's eternal care.

So let the hymn resound,
throughout the world around,
for we are healed and whole,
in mercy's warm control.

Beneath the Veil of Pain

Beneath the veil of pain,
hope whispers, soft as rain,
every tear casts a prayer,
lifting burdens we bear.

Through the shadows that enclose,
a light of grace still glows,
illuminating the way,
guiding us day by day.

In the depths of our night,
we cling to the true light,
with each heartbeat we strive,
celebrating the alive.

For suffering's heavy hand,
teaches us to understand,
that in each heavy sigh,
we learn how to rise high.

So let us dance through the dark,
finding joy in every spark,
for beneath the veil of pain,
hope and love will remain.

The Seed of Struggle

In shadows deep, a seed does lie,
With whispered hopes, it seeks the sky.
Through pain and strife, it learns to grow,
The light it bends, the love it knows.

Each tear that falls, a drop of grace,
Nurturing roots in this holy place.
From broken dreams, new paths arise,
Awakening strength, beneath the skies.

Grit and faith, the farmer's tools,
In yielding earth, the Spirit rules.
For every storm that tests the heart,
A bolder seed shall take its part.

With every struggle, purpose found,
In darkest nights, the stars surround.
So let us toil and let us strive,
For in each trial, we come alive.

And when the harvest time draws near,
We'll gather love, release our fear.
The seed of struggle, strong and free,
Is blessed by grace, eternally.

Blessings Born of Trials

From ashes rise, a story told,
In trials faced, our hearts grow bold.
Each burden bears a sacred weight,
In patience learned, we open fate.

The stormy seas, they crash and roar,
Yet in the depths, we seek to soar.
With every wave that pulls us under,
We find the light beyond the thunder.

For in our wounds, the light comes through,
A testament to what is true.
Blessings born from darkest night,
Are forged in faith and endless light.

So when we stumble, when we fall,
We rise again, we heed the call.
For trials lead to strength divine,
Our spirits shine, our souls align.

With open hearts, we gather grace,
Transforming struggles into space.
A life renewed, with each embrace,
Reflections of our sacred place.

Through the Valley of the Scarred

Through valleys dark, our journey winds,
With scarred and weary hearts aligned.
Each step we take, though filled with pain,
Brings wisdom deep, like gentle rain.

In echoes lost, we hear the call,
Of broken souls, divinely small.
Yet in their fractures, beauty shines,
The love of God, through space and time.

We walk together, side by side,
Through rugged paths, where dreams abide.
With faith ignited, hope restored,
We lift our voices, hearts adored.

In barren lands, where shadows tread,
We plant our seeds, where angels led.
For every sorrow, every scar,
Is proof of light that guides us far.

So let us rise, while shadows cower,
With faith as strong as sacred power.
Through valleys rough, we find our way,
With grace bestowed, we seize the day.

Rising from Ruins

From crumbled walls, new visions sprout,
In wreckage found, we learn about.
Each fractured beam, a tale to tell,
Of strength reborn, from depths of hell.

The ashes breathe, with winds of change,
In brokenness, we rearrange.
With guiding hands and hopeful eyes,
We build anew where lost dreams lie.

Through every fall, we learn to stand,
In unity, we craft and plan.
For every ruin holds the key,
To depths of love and clarity.

With hearts aflame, we rise again,
Transforming losses into gain.
Through trials faced, and lessons learned,
The spirit's fire forever burned.

So let us lift, what once was lost,
In rising from our steady cost.
For from the ruins, new lives bloom,
In every heart, dispelling gloom.

The Anointed Burden

Upon the sacred paths we tread,
With weary hearts and voices led.
The weight of grace upon our backs,
In whispered prayers, we find no lack.

In shadows cast, our spirits rise,
The anointed cry, the faithful sighs.
With every step, we bear the flame,
A testament to His great name.

Through trials faced and battles won,
We carry hope like endless sun.
For in our burdens, love resides,
Anointed hearts, our faith abides.

In valleys low, our dreams take flight,
The sacred truth our guiding light.
Embrace the weight, it shapes our soul,
A humble heart will find its whole.

So let us walk as one divine,
Together in this love, we shine.
For in the burden, purpose grows,
The anointed path, where mercy flows.

Journey Through the Valley of Shadows

In valleys deep where shadows dwell,
We walk the path, we trust, we tell.
A journey marked by faith and grace,
Each step we take, He takes our place.

Through whispers dark and fears collide,
Our souls are bound, in Him we bide.
Beyond the shadows, light will break,
A promise true, for His name's sake.

With heavy hearts, we rise anew,
In every tear, His love shines through.
The valley's song, a haunting tune,
Yet in His arms, we find our boon.

When hope seems lost and nights are long,
We gather strength, we sing our song.
For every shadow has a light,
In darkest hours, we find our sight.

So onward march, we face the night,
In every struggle, seek the light.
A journey forged in faith's embrace,
Through valleys low, we find His grace.

Hymns of Healing

In every wound, a hymn is sung,
Of healing grace, forever young.
With gentle hands, He binds the sore,
A melody that sings restore.

Our broken hearts, a sacred place,
Within the pain, we seek His face.
The balm of love, a soothing thread,
In every tear, His mercy spread.

Come weary souls, lay down your fears,
In harmony we share our tears.
A hymn of hope, a sacred dance,
In healing light, we take our chance.

With every note, the spirit soars,
In troubled times, His peace restores.
Through hymns of healing, hearts align,
In joyful song, our spirits shine.

So raise your voice, let praises ring,
For in His arms, our souls take wing.
Through hymns of healing, love prevails,
A promise kept, where faith exhales.

Mosaic of the Afflicted

In fractured dreams and scattered hope,
We piece our hearts, learn how to cope.
A mosaic bright of pain and grace,
In every shard, His light we trace.

Each story told, a tender thread,
Through wounds endured, a life well-read.
Together bound, we rise anew,
In every flaw, His love breaks through.

The art of healing, complex and rare,
In brokenness, we learn to care.
A tapestry of souls entwined,
In every heart, His truth defined.

So let us gather, hand in hand,
A mosaic rich, together stand.
For in the ache, we find our song,
In unity, we all belong.

From darkest nights to brightest days,
We weave a culture of His ways.
Together we, the afflicted share,
A living art, a love laid bare.

Blessings from the Battle

In the storm, I found my grace,
Through the struggle, I sought Your face.
Shields raised high, we stand as one,
In the fight, Your will be done.

Voices raised in sacred song,
Together we are ever strong.
With every scar, Your love bestowed,
In battle's heart, our faith unfolds.

The armor shines, a testament,
To trials faced and lives well-spent.
With faith like fire, we forge ahead,
In every step, our spirits fed.

In the fray, we find the truth,
Hearts of warriors in brutal youth.
In prayer, we share the burdens deep,
For in Your light, our souls will leap.

From ashes rise, a holy breath,
In life's cruel dance, we conquer death.
Each challenge met, a path divine,
In every battle, Your love will shine.

The Pilgrim's Pain

With weary feet, the journey long,
In shadows cast, my heart stays strong.
Each step I take, a silent plea,
O guide my soul, let me be free.

Through valleys low and mountains steep,
In heartache's grasp, my burdens keep.
Yet still I move, though it is hard,
With faith as my ever-watchful guard.

The road is rough, the night is dark,
Yet in my soul, You leave a mark.
In every tear, a lesson learned,
With every fall, Your love returned.

The weight I bear, a sacred gift,
In pain, my spirit starts to lift.
A pilgrim's heart, both brave and wise,
Sees beauty in the breaking skies.

In every ache, Your promise found,
A hope renewed, where faith abounds.
Through trials faced, my soul ascends,
In pilgrimage, the journey bends.

The Light Through the Cracks

In shadows cast by weary days,
Your light breaks forth in brilliant rays.
Through fractures deep in humble ground,
In every crack, Your grace is found.

The broken heart, the wounded soul,
In every gap, You make it whole.
A flicker here, a spark revealed,
Your love and mercy are our shield.

From shattered dreams and hopes once lost,
We rise again, though pain's the cost.
With every tear, a story told,
In fractured lives, Your hand we hold.

When darkness looms and shadows breathe,
Your shining light begins to weave.
A tapestry of faith and grace,
In every crack, Your warm embrace.

Through all the trials that we face,
In every scar, Your light will grace.
For even in the darkest night,
We find our hope through cracks of light.

Sacrificial Tattoos

Inked on skin, the stories run,
Each mark a battle, every one.
A life lived deep, with scars displayed,
In sacrificial love conveyed.

Every line a moment penned,
In struggles fought and foes we fend.
A witness bold of grace profound,
In pain and beauty, truth is found.

These etchings speak of journeys past,
Of faith and hope, forever cast.
In agony, a purpose grows,
In every stain, Your mercy glows.

With every ink, a prayer released,
On this canvas, fears decreased.
A testament of trials faced,
In sacrificial love embraced.

Through ink and proof, my spirit sings,
In every scar, the joy it brings.
For through my pain, I've come to know,
In sacred art, Your love will flow.

Forging Faith

In the quiet night, we seek the light,
Voices whisper hope, banishing fright.
With each trial faced, our spirits rise,
In the forge of grace, wisdom lies.

Hands raised in prayer, we find our strength,
In the depths of love, we go the length.
Bound by the heart, the soul does soar,
In faith, we stand, united in more.

Through shadows deep, we walk the way,
Guided by truth, we choose to stay.
In every struggle, a blessing's born,
From ashes we rise, a new day sworn.

The journey long, yet hearts ablaze,
For in the trials, we sing His praise.
With every breath, a sacred trust,
In God we find, our love is just.

Forged in the fire, steadfast and true,
A legacy bright, in all that we do.
Through tempest and storm, we find our peace,
In the arms of grace, our fears shall cease.

Tides of Affliction

In the crashing waves of life's despair,
We find the echoes of earnest prayer.
The tide may rise, yet we hold fast,
For through the storm, we are steadfast.

Each tear we shed, a river flows,
In sorrow's depth, compassion grows.
When shadows loom and darkness spreads,
In faith we stand, our spirit led.

Count not your troubles, but your grace,
For every trial has its place.
In pain's embrace, we learn to heal,
Through love's sweet whisper, we reveal.

Across the dunes of barren land,
The heart of God is close at hand.
In every struggle, the spirit's song,
In harmony with life, we belong.

So as the tide ebbs and flows,
In every heart, a light still glows.
For in affliction, we are made whole,
In suffering's fire, we find the soul.

The Canvas of Experience

Life paints its strokes in vibrant hues,
With every brush, a tale to choose.
Through laughter's joy and sorrow's pain,
A masterpiece forged, not in vain.

Each moment a thread in the grand design,
Woven with purpose, a love divine.
In shadows cast and light revealed,
The heart's true canvas remains unsealed.

We gather colors from days gone by,
In triumph and loss, we learn to fly.
With faith as our guide, through dark and bright,
We paint our journey in love's pure light.

Through every heartache, the artist flows,
Crafting our path as the spirit knows.
In the gallery of life, we stand tall,
In unity's grace, we'll conquer all.

So let us adorn this canvas wide,
With hues of hope that never hide.
For in every layer, our truth unfolds,
A testament of love, in stories told.

Revelations from the Ruined

In the ashes of what once was whole,
We find the fragments, we find the soul.
In brokenness, God's promise shines,
Amidst the ruins, His love aligns.

The shattered dreams, like stars anew,
From darkness rise, a brilliant hue.
In every fracture, His light breaks through,
In every pain, a vision true.

We gather stones from the paths we weave,
In the silence, we learn to believe.
With every tear, the spirit mends,
In broken places, our journey bends.

Through crumbled walls, hope still stands strong,
In the heart's deep well, we find our song.
For from the ruins of grief and loss,
We learn to bear, we learn the cross.

So let the heart's whispers guide the way,
In shattered places, we'll find our play.
For every ruin holds a promise bright,
In the depth of night, we choose the light.

The Joy of the Journey

With each step we walk in grace,
Embraced by love, we find our place.
Through valleys low and mountains high,
We lift our hearts, we touch the sky.

In every trial, faith will glow,
A gentle whisper guides us so.
With open eyes, we see the light,
The joy of journey, pure and bright.

Hand in hand, we share the road,
The burdens light, the love bestowed.
In every moment, cherish all,
Together we shall never fall.

With laughter sweet, and praises sung,
A melody of hope, we've strung.
In unity, our spirits soar,
The joy of life, forevermore.

So onward march, with hearts aflame,
In love and peace, we stake our claim.
With every heartbeat, trust we'll weave,
The joy of journey, we'll believe.

Holy Resilience

Amidst the storms that fiercely blow,
We stand upright, with spirits aglow.
Steadfast we rise, though shadows loom,
For in our hearts, there lies a bloom.

Each scar a testament of grace,
A holy light, our saving trace.
In trials faced, we find our worth,
Resilience born from sacred earth.

When doubt encroaches, we will fight,
With faith as shield, we seek the light.
In whispered prayers, our strength renewed,
Holy resilience, our gratitude.

Together bound in love's embrace,
We find the courage to believe.
In every struggle, hope ignites,
A holy fire that never bites.

So rise, dear souls, and tread the path,
In unity, we defeat the wrath.
With arms outstretched, we shall proclaim,
Holy resilience, forever flame.

Unveiling Inner Strength

In silence deep, a voice will rise,
A soul awakened, truth's disguise.
Through darkness thick, our spirits roam,
Unveiling strength, we find our home.

With every doubt that clouds the mind,
The light within is what we'll find.
Compassion's heart beats strong and true,
In every challenge, we break through.

Beneath the weight of wounding fears,
The courage grows, dissolving tears.
In sacred space, we stand as one,
Unveiling strength, the battle won.

Embrace the light that shines within,
No longer shackled by our sin.
With open hearts, we dare to trust,
Unveiling strength, it's more than just.

So rise with love, and take the leap,
In every breath, our souls we keep.
With faith as guide, we journey long,
Unveiling strength, our sacred song.

Sanctuary of the Scarred

In every wound, a story told,
A sanctuary for the bold.
Through trials faced and battles fought,
The scars we bear are not for naught.

In broken places, light shines through,
Healing whispers, soft and true.
A refuge built on love's embrace,
Sanctuary found in sacred space.

Each mark a lesson, each tear a gift,
In every heartbeat, spirits lift.
Together held in love's embrace,
Sanctuary of the scarred, our place.

With open arms, we welcome all,
In faith and hope, we heed the call.
In unity, we rise and stand,
Sanctuary of the scarred, so grand.

So carry forth this truth we share,
In every heart, we find the care.
With every story, hear the sound,
Sanctuary of the scarred, we've found.

Mending the Spirit's Fabric

In silence, the heart begins to mend,
Threads of hope in shadows blend,
With every tear, a story sewn,
Divine hands cradle the broken stone.

The fabric of faith is gently pulled,
Hearts are healed, and fears are lulled,
In whispers soft, the spirit sings,
Of love unbound, and holy things.

Each stitch a prayer, a sacred plea,
Woven into the tapestry,
A tapestry of grace and light,
Worn proudly through the darkest night.

Through every gap, the light shall flow,
Bringing warmth wherever we go,
With every heartache softly quelled,
In the fabric of spirit, hope is held.

So mend we must, with gentle hands,
In unity, our faith expands,
For together we create the whole,
Mending the fabric of every soul.

Chiseled by the Hands of Time

In the quarry of days, we are shaped,
Carved by trials, no moment escaped,
Edges worn, yet smooth we stand,
Chiseled with care, by a master's hand.

Each scar a story, each crease a tale,
Weathered by storms, yet we prevail,
In the currents of time, we find our way,
Guided by faith through night and day.

With patience, we learn, we grow and bend,
Facing the trials, we seek to ascend,
For in the chisel, a beauty lies,
Reflecting the grace of the endless skies.

In moments of stillness, we hear the call,
To rise above and never fall,
For time is the sculptor—the hands divine,
Molding our essence, our spirits align.

As the stone reveals what's hidden within,
So do we flourish, forgiven of sin,
Chiseled by love, so strong and true,
In the arms of time, we are born anew.

Songs of the Scarred

In shadows deep, a melody waits,
The songs of the scarred, soft serenades,
With every note, the pain we share,
Binding our hearts, in love and care.

Each battle fought, each wound embraced,
Turns sorrow to strength, forever graced,
For in the scars, a beauty unfolds,
A testament of courage, a story told.

We gather our voices, a chorus strong,
In unity we rise, where we belong,
With chords of hope, we lift each other,
In the songs of the scarred, we find our mother.

Through valleys low and mountains high,
We sing our dreams into the sky,
For in our hearts, the light shall beam,
In songs of the scarred, we dare to dream.

So let the echoes ring far and wide,
With every scar, let love abide,
For redemption rings, and healing starts,
In the joyous songs of our scarred hearts.

Transcendence Through Tears

In the silence of sorrow, a river flows,
Transcendence awaits where the heartache grows,
For every tear that falls from grace,
A journey begins, a sacred space.

Each drop a prayer, released to the night,
In vulnerability, we find the light,
Through cracks of despair, hope finds a way,
Transcending the darkness, a brand new day.

Cleansed by the rain, our spirits renew,
In the embrace of love, we rise and pursue,
For tears are the wings that carry our soul,
To heights unimagined, we become whole.

In every sorrow, a lesson to gain,
Transcendence unfolds from our deepest pain,
With each tear shed, the heart learns to soar,
Embracing the blessings life has in store.

So let us weep, for beauty is near,
In the depths of sadness, we conquer fear,
Transcendence is found in the grace of the fall,
Through tears, we awaken, answering the call.

Embers of Faith Rising

In the shadows, faith ignites,
Whispers of hope take flight.
Through trials, our hearts soar,
Embers glow, forevermore.

In the dark, a light gleams,
Guiding us through silent screams.
With every tear, we find grace,
In the ashes, love's embrace.

Beneath the burden, spirits shine,
In suffering, we intertwine.
Together, our spirits rise,
Boundless under open skies.

From the depths, our voices call,
Resurrected, we stand tall.
Faith like fire, fierce and bright,
Warming souls in endless night.

Through the toil, we seek the dawn,
With hope alive, we journey on.
Embers spark a mighty flame,
In our hearts, the sacred name.

Divine Beauty in the Broken

In the cracks, grace finds its way,
Through brokenness, we learn to pray.
Pieces shattered, still they shine,
In the chaos, love divine.

Each scar tells a sacred tale,
In our wounds, the spirit sails.
Beauty blooms amidst the tears,
In our weakness, strength appears.

Voices lifted, souls unite,
Finding peace in shared plight.
Hearts entwined, we rise anew,
Through the storms, our faith rings true.

In the shadows, beauty gleams,
In broken hearts, we find dreams.
Hand in hand, we walk the way,
In love's light, we choose to stay.

From the wreckage, life is born,
With every dusk, there comes the morn.
In the silence, divinity hums,
Through the broken, holy comes.

Sacred Paths of the Wounded

On sacred ground, the wounded tread,
With every step, our spirits led.
Paths of grace, though strained and worn,
Through the hurt, new hope is born.

Each stumble, a lesson learned,
In the fire, our souls are burned.
Yet through pain, we find our way,
In the night, we see the day.

Together, we share the load,
In the broken, love bestowed.
Hearts as one, we rise and sway,
Finding strength in what we say.

Amidst the hurt, the spirit thrives,
In every pulse, the truth arrives.
Wounded, yet we stand so tall,
In love's embrace, we cannot fall.

While shadows dance upon the earth,
In our trials, we find our worth.
With each wound, compassion grows,
Sacred paths where healing flows.

Celestial Echoes of Agony

In the silence, voices cry,
Celestial echoes fill the sky.
Every tear a star that falls,
Agony in sacred calls.

From the depths, the pain ascends,
In our hearts, the journey bends.
Light and dark, they intertwine,
In the agony, the divine.

Hope emerges from the night,
In our struggles, our true light.
Melodies of sorrow play,
In the night, they pave the way.

Through the hurt, we hear the song,
In every note, we still belong.
Celestial whispers guide the way,
In our anguish, prayers convey.

And so we rise, from pain to peace,
In the echoes, our fears cease.
Celestial hearts, forever strong,
In the agony, we find our song.

Beautified by Battle

In the furnace of trial, we arise,
With hearts ablaze, reaching for the skies.
Each scar a story, each wound divine,
In battles fought, our spirits entwine.

The storm may rage, the night may fall,
Yet through the darkness, we heed the call.
A warrior's grace, a steadfast heart,
From ashes of struggle, we will not part.

In every struggle, a lesson learned,
Through tempest and toil, our faith is burned.
The beauty of courage, in silence borne,
In beautified battle, we are reborn.

With prayer as our shield, and hope as our sword,
We march through the shadows, trusting the Lord.
In every setback, we find our way,
A tapestry woven, night turns to day.

So stand together, let voices rise,
In unity's strength, we pierce the skies.
For those who battle shall wear the crown,
Beautified by struggle, we shall not drown.

Embracing the Imperfect

In the mirror's gaze, truth sets us free,
With flaws and fractures, we learn to be.
Each crack a story, each shadow a guide,
In the arms of the flawed, love will abide.

For life's perfect moments are seldom found,
In the symphony of chaos, joy can resound.
Each stumble, each rise, a dance of the soul,
In embracing the imperfect, we find our whole.

Beneath the surface, beauty unfolds,
In the hands of the broken, a treasure behold.
With compassion as our compass, we tread the way,
Finding grace in the shadows, come what may.

So let us gather our hearts, hand in hand,
With hopes intertwined, we bravely stand.
For in our shared journeys, we deeply connect,
Embracing the imperfect, we're never defect.

In the sacred space of vulnerability laid,
Love finds its roots in the flaws we've made.
Together we flourish, amidst every wrong,
In the tapestry woven, we all belong.

Prayers Woven in Pain

In whispers of sorrow, our prayers are sewn,
With aching hearts, we're never alone.
In the tapestry woven of struggle's embrace,
Prayers rise like incense, finding their place.

Each tear a river, each sigh a plea,
In the depths of our anguish, we long to be free.
Yet through the shadows, our voices will blend,
Woven in pain, we rise and ascend.

In the night's quiet still, hope flickers bright,
With faith as our armor, we embrace the fight.
For every battle cloaked in despair,
Our prayers woven tightly, connect us in care.

So let the winds carry our songs to the skies,
In the strength of our spirits, our love never dies.
Through brokenness blooming, our hearts will remain,
In the symphony of life, our prayers woven in pain.

For God walks beside us in valleys profound,
In the echoes of struggle, His love will abound.
With each whispered prayer, we heal and we gain,
In the beauty of solace, we rise through the rain.

Strength Amidst the Strain

When burdens weigh heavy, and skies turn gray,
In the midst of the strain, we find our way.
With every heartbeat, resilience takes flight,
Strength amid struggles, a guiding light.

In the valley of shadows, where fears align,
Hope lingers quietly, a sacred sign.
For where the heart trembles, the spirit ignites,
In strength amidst strain, we embrace the fights.

Each challenge we face, a step toward the dawn,
With courage our armor, we'll carry on.
For in every struggle, our faith will refine,
In the depths of despair, our souls brightly shine.

So lift up your gaze, let your worries release,
In the rhythm of faith, we'll find our peace.
For together we stand, united as one,
Strength amidst the strain, our battles are won.

With every heartbeat, let love be our guide,
In the journey of life, we'll walk side by side.
For in the embrace of the trials, we'll learn,
In strength amid strain, our spirits will burn.

Pilgrimage to Perseverance

In the silence of the dawn, we tread,
With faith as our guide, we forge ahead.
Each step a whisper, each breath a prayer,
Through valleys of doubt, we rise from despair.

The path may be rugged, the journey long,
Yet in the struggle, we find our song.
Hearts intertwined, seeking the light,
In shadows we bask, in grace we unite.

With every heartbeat, strength is renewed,
Courage ignites in the hearts of the few.
For every stumble, we gather our might,
In the pilgrimage's night, we find our light.

The mountains before us, tall and profound,
In the stillness, our voices resound.
Together we march, onward we strive,
In this sacred journey, we come alive.

At the end of the road, the truth shall unveil,
The beauty of spirit that cannot fail.
For in every trial, there's a lesson learned,
In the fires of challenge, our faith is burned.

The Beauty of the Shattered

In brokenness lies the truth of our heart,
Shattered pieces play their part.
From ashes and dust we rise and we bloom,
In the ruins of sorrow, we find room.

Each crack a story, each scar a song,
In the tapestry woven, where we belong.
For beauty emerges from pain's gentle kiss,
In the chaos of life, we find our bliss.

The light shines bright through the fractured night,
Illuminating paths with its sacred might.
In the dance of the fallen, we learn to forgive,
In embracing the shards, we truly live.

With each shattered dream, a new hope ignites,
A testament of courage that soars to great heights.
From the depths of despair, to the wings of the soul,
In the beauty of brokenness, we become whole.

So cherish the fragments, the lessons they bear,
In the symphony played, find joy in the air.
For life in its splendor is both wild and sweet,
In the beauty of shattered, our spirits meet.

Radiance from Ruin

Amidst the rubble, stars shine clear,
In the remnants of darkness, hope draws near.
Each fragment of night holds a promise bright,
In the depths of despair, there blooms the light.

The echoes of silence, a soft lullaby,
Remind us of strength as we reach for the sky.
From the ruins of doubt, faith takes its flight,
Radiance rising, fierce and bright.

In the heart of the storm, where shadows may play,
We learn to find peace, to find our own way.
Through trials and turmoils, we gather our grace,
In the spirit of love, we find our place.

Though valleys are deep and mountains are steep,
With courage as anchor, our dreams we'll keep.
For no ruin can sever what the heart knows true,
In the radiance flowing, we are renewed.

So stand in the rubble, embrace the call,
For from what was broken, we shall not fall.
Together united, we rise from the gloom,
With radiance shining, we'll conquer our doom.

Prayers in the Cracks

In the spaces where hope seems thin,
We gather our fears, let prayers begin.
With hearts wide open, we whisper our pleas,
In the cracks of our sorrow, a spirit that frees.

For every fracture, a prayer finds its way,
Illuminating shadows, bringing forth day.
In the silence we gather, in the stillness we hear,
The echoes of faith that draw us near.

When burdens grow heavy and paths are unclear,
In the cracks of our struggles, we sense You near.
With each cry for mercy, with every lament,
In the shelter of grace, our hearts are content.

The beauty of being, both fragile and bold,
In the prayers of the broken, new stories unfold.
From crumbling foundations, new life will arise,
With prayers in the cracks, we soar to the skies.

So let us embrace what the weary may find,
In the depths of despair, our spirits aligned.
With love overflowing, we rise from our plight,
In the light of our prayers, we reclaim our light.

Echoes of Endurance

In quiet realms where faith unfolds,
The heart resounds with tales of old.
Through valleys deep and mountains high,
I seek the light beyond the sky.

With every tear, a lesson blooms,
In shadows cast by life's dark rooms.
A whispered prayer, a steadfast stand,
Guided gently by His hand.

The strength within, a quiet roar,
Resumes its pace; I push for more.
For trials faced are stones of grace,
A steadfast, ever-holy place.

Each stumble brings me closer still,
To understanding Heaven's will.
In sacred echoes, hope's refrain,
I rise anew from deepest pain.

And as I walk this path of light,
I find my way in darkest night.
Faith is the bridge that never breaks,
In every challenge, joy awakes.

The Altar of Affliction

Upon the altar, burdens lie,
A testament to faith's fierce cry.
With every wound, I find a way,
To praise the storms that led to sway.

In suffering's grip, my spirit grows,
A garden blooms where anguish flows.
Each prayer a seed, with love I sow,
Trusting the path where He might go.

The darkness whispers strength unseen,
In battles fought, I reign supreme.
The light within, a beacon bright,
Illuminates the longest night.

Through trials hot as furnace flame,
I learn to carry love's pure name.
With every scar, a story told,
In quiet times, the heart grows bold.

So let me stand, though shaken, torn,
In grace renewed, I am reborn.
The altar stands, a place to yield,
A sacred ground where truth is sealed.

Divine Testimony

In every struggle, wisdom speaks,
The truth emerging through the peaks.
A faithful heart, though bruised and weak,
Holds to the promise, seeks to speak.

With every challenge, I comply,
To see the world through sacred eye.
The storms may rage, the night may fall,
Yet echoes of His love enthrall.

In trials passed, I find my voice,
In pain endured, I see the choice.
To lift my hands, to shout His name,
In life's great dance, I'm not the same.

The testimony of my years,
Is written through both joy and tears.
For in the battles, I've discerned,
The fire refines, the heart has turned.

A sanctified, enduring flight,
I rise and soar, embrace the light.
Each moment carved in faith and love,
A divine testament above.

Inked by Trials

With ink of trials, my story's penned,
Each chapter a struggle, a message to send.
From ashes to beauty, my scars are drawn,
The tale of survival, at the break of dawn.

Amidst the tempest, I sought His grace,
Finding my refuge in sacred space.
The pages turn with lessons learned,
In darkest nights, my spirit burned.

Through valleys low and mountains steep,
The promise kept, a path to reap.
With faith as my compass, I journey on,
Inked by trials, my heart has grown strong.

Each sorrow faced, a brush with light,
Transforming shadows into sight.
What once was pain, now hope reframed,
In every struggle, love proclaimed.

So flow the words, with courage bold,
Recorded in time, a truth to hold.
My life a canvas, crafted anew,
Inked by trials, forever true.

In the Shadow of Redemption

In the quiet hour, grace descends,
Washing souls, where darkness bends.
Hearts in anguish, seeking light,
In shadows deep, we find our might.

Whispers of hope, the angels sing,
Through trials faced, redemption brings.
Faith like a river, flowing free,
In its embrace, we come to be.

Every tear, a sacred gift,
In brokenness, our spirits lift.
Through stormy nights, the dawn will rise,
In shadow's depth, our spirits fly.

Forgiveness seeds in fertile ground,
Where love abides, grace can be found.
Embrace the journey, trust the way,
In redemption's arms, we long to stay.

A light that conquers, pure and bright,
In the shadow, we find our fight.
Forged in trials, our spirits soar,
In the shadow of redemption, evermore.

Threads Woven by Pain

In every stitch, a story told,
Threads of sorrow, woven bold.
Pain like a needle, piercing deep,
Through every struggle, our hearts leap.

Tears like raindrops fall anew,
In weaving light, we find what's true.
Crafted by hands that know the cost,
In every loss, we gather, not lost.

Embroidered hopes, in darkness dawn,
With every thread, a new life's drawn.
In the fabric of faith, we intertwine,
Through pain's embrace, our spirits shine.

The tapestry of life unfolds,
In threads of pain, our truth behold.
Stitched with courage, stitched with grace,
In every wound, a holy place.

We wear our scars as crowns of light,
In woven fibers, we unite.
Threads of suffering, threads of grace,
In a world torn, we find our place.

Epistles of Endurance

In letters penned with faith's own hand,
Through trials faced, we make our stand.
Each struggle met, a message sent,
In epistles of love, we find content.

Words of wisdom, in silence lie,
A testament to the reasons why.
In storms we write, our truths declared,
Endurance blooms where hearts are bared.

Each page a mirror, reflecting pain,
In every loss, new strength we gain.
Message of hope, through shadows cast,
In every moment, a prayer, steadfast.

With ink of faith, we draft our lives,
In each endurance, the spirit thrives.
A journey shared, we write our song,
In unity found, we all belong.

In every chapter, His grace unfolds,
Through battles won, our truth upholds.
Epistles bound in love's embrace,
In every struggle, we find His grace.

The Altar of Suffering

At the altar of suffering, hearts lay bare,
In trials endured, we find our prayer.
Sacrifices made, with each tear shed,
In the crucible of pain, our hopes are fed.

Gathered in faith, we stand as one,
In shadows deep, new life begun.
The price of love, through blood and fire,
On this altar, we raise our choir.

Through every wound, a lesson learned,
In suffering's forge, our spirits burned.
But from the ash, we rise anew,
At the altar of suffering, truth shines through.

Each scar a story, each bruise a song,
For in our weakness, we grow strong.
United in grief, we find our peace,
From this altar, blessings never cease.

To suffer is to love, to bear the strain,
Through every sorrow, we break the chain.
In the heart of pain, our spirits sing,
At the altar of suffering, hope takes wing.

The Grace Found in Grief

In shadows deep, we find our way,
Through tears that fall, we learn to pray.
Each sorrow bears a sacred seed,
In mourning's grasp, our spirits lead.

The darkness whispers, hope will rise,
A gentle light in sorrow's guise.
With every loss, a treasure gained,
In grief, the heart is gently trained.

The echo of a love once near,
Transforms the pain, our eyes must clear.
A loving hand, though lost to sight,
Now guides us through the endless night.

In silent moments, truth is shown,
From grief's embrace, we are not alone.
The grace bestowed teaches to hold,
The warmth of love, brighter than gold.

Though heavy burdens we must bear,
The hope of dawn is always there.
With hearts alight, we walk anew,
For in our grief, we find what's true.

From Ashes to Anointment

From ashes cold, a flame set free,
In darkest night, a spark we see.
With humble hearts, we rise and stand,
Renewed by love's compassionate hand.

The past may fade like whispers lost,
Yet through the fire, we count the cost.
In every trial, a lesson learned,
A brighter path from sorrow earned.

Anointed now by trials faced,
We find our strength in love embraced.
With faith as guide, we turn the page,
And from our pain, we disengage.

In sacred bonds, our spirits weave,
A tapestry we dare believe.
From grief's embrace, new life begins,
In ashes born, our journey spins.

Resilience blooms, like flowers bright,
From darkest depths, we find the light.
The heart rejoiced, though heavy still,
In every moment, God's sweet will.

The Celestial Currency of Trials

In trials faced, our spirits grow,
Each challenge met, a gift to sow.
Through every storm, we find our way,
A currency of grace, we pray.

The struggles teach, they mold our soul,
In hardship's grip, we find the whole.
Though weary hearts may tremble still,
Within the struggle, find God's will.

Each scar adorned becomes a mark,
Reminders of the light in dark.
With every trial, a story spun,
In moments shared, our souls are one.

The weight we bear, a heavy price,
But in that cost, we see the spice.
For in the trials, love's truth is found,
A melody that knows no bound.

With open hearts, we learn to see,
The currency of trials, free.
In brokenness, we find the song,
Our sacred dance, where we belong.

Unveiling the Sacred Story

In every heart, a tale untold,
In whispered dreams, the truth unfolds.
Through trials faced and blessings shared,
The sacred story, love declared.

Each chapter written, inked in tears,
With faith, we face our deepest fears.
In every heartbeat, grace revealed,
A journey vast, our hearts unsealed.

The pages turn, we grasp the pen,
In unity, we rise again.
With open arms, the light breaks through,
A sacred path for me and you.

From scars we bear, our strength will grow,
In love's embrace, together, flow.
With every sunrise, fresh starts bloom,
Transforming darkness into room.

Unveiling now, the sacred truth,
In search of joy, reclaim our youth.
Together woven, we give glory,
In every life, unfolds the story.

The Testament of our Trials

In the valley of shadows we tread,
With faith our guiding light ahead.
Each trial a lesson, every tear we sow,
In the garden of strength, our spirits grow.

Chains of despair we patiently break,
For in each burden, our souls awake.
Through fire and storm, we raise our song,
In the arms of the Almighty, we truly belong.

Though mountains loom and rivers roar,
His mercy shines, forevermore.
With every heartbeat and silent prayer,
We find His presence, always there.

In the echoes of anguish, hope is found,
In whispered promises, love unbound.
Our testament of trials stands tall,
A chorus of courage answering the call.

Through valleys low and peaks so high,
We walk with Him, our spirits fly.
Our trials a testament, hearts aflame,
In the book of our lives, we write His name.

Blessings Born from the Battle

In the clash of swords and fervent fight,
We find the blessings, shining bright.
For every wound, a story we tell,
In the heart of our struggle, we find our well.

With courage as armor, we take our stand,
In the heat of the battle, united we band.
Through sacrifice and strife, we rise,
A tapestry woven beneath sacred skies.

Through darkest nights and fiercest storms,
In His embrace, our spirit warms.
Each wound a chapter, each scar a grace,
In the fight for love, we find our place.

From ashes we rise, like phoenixes fly,
In the depths of despair, we breathe the sky.
Blessings born, from the battles we face,
In the light of His mercy, we find our space.

With hearts unyielding and visions clear,
We march forth boldly, casting out fear.
For every battle, a blessing bestowed,
In faith's fulfillment, our spirits erode.

In the legacy forged through turmoil and strain,
We gather the lessons, embrace the pain.
For the blessings of battle in Christ we see,
A triumph of love, setting hearts free.

Grace in the Grief

In the shadows of sorrow, we find our way,
With grace in our hearts, we choose to stay.
Though tears may fall and spirits break,
In every heartbeat, our faith we wake.

Through valleys of loss, we walk alone,
Yet in each whisper, His love is shown.
In the embrace of sorrow, we learn to stand,
With grace as our anchor, held in His hand.

Though the night is long and hope seems far,
His gentle light shines like a star.
In the depths of grief, we find a song,
A melody woven, where we belong.

With every memory, a thread of love,
In the tapestry of life, woven above.
Grace in the grief, a bittersweet gift,
We rise from the ashes, as spirits lift.

For in our sorrow, He walks with grace,
With every heartbeat, we find our place.
In the arms of His mercy, we heal and grow,
In the journey of grief, His light we know.

The Bodies of Our Testimonies

In the gathering of souls, we share our plight,
The bodies of our stories, shining bright.
With scars like badges, we proclaim our fight,
In the warmth of fellowship, we ignite the light.

Each heartbeat echoes the truth we bear,
In the chorus of our trials, love and care.
Through the stories we tell, and voices we raise,
We become a testament, a song of praise.

With arms open wide, we embrace the pain,
For in every struggle, there is much to gain.
In the bodies of our testimonies, strong,
We find our belonging where we all belong.

In the tapestry woven, our stories entwine,
The grace of the Lord in every line.
For every mountain climbed and every fall,
In unity we stand, answering the call.

Each life's a vessel, a story divine,
In the heart of the faithful, His love will shine.
Together we walk, with joy we proceed,
In the bodies of our testimonies, we are freed.

The Light in the Shadows

In the depths, where darkness looms,
A flicker shines, dispelling glooms.
With faith as guide, hearts are bold,
A promise whispered, truths retold.

The shadows cast, they cannot stay,
For grace will chase the night away.
In quiet prayer, the soul ascends,
Where light and love eternally blend.

Around the cross, the shadows flee,
In every heart, there's victory.
With every tear, a lesson learned,
Through faith and hope, the soul returned.

In trials faced, we stand the test,
With courage strong, we find our rest.
The light ignites the sacred fire,
A beacon bright, our one desire.

Embrace the light that pierces night,
In every soul, His truth ignites.
From shadows deep, we rise anew,
In faith and love, we find our view.

Redemption in the Raw

In brokenness, there lies a grace,
A chance to seek a higher place.
Through scars and pain, the heart will know,
Redemption blooms where shadows grow.

From ashes rise the voices strong,
In unity, we sing His song.
The chains that bind now fall away,
In Christ alone, we find our way.

The raw and real, in truth we stand,
Embracing all, with open hands.
In every fall, a lesson found,
With every tear, His love abounds.

The journey fraught with thorns and light,
Through deepest valleys, we take flight.
In surrender, we find our peace,
A grace that brings the soul's release.

Hope rises high, though tempests roar,
In every heart, He opens doors.
Embrace the storm, the lessons raw,
Through trials faced, we see His law.

Chronicles of the Wounded

Within our wounds, the stories dwell,
Of battles fought, of pain to tell.
In every heart, a passage scribed,
Chronicles of love, we imbibe.

The wounded rise, their voices strong,
In unity, we all belong.
With every scar, a tale of grace,
In brokenness, we find our place.

In gentle whispers, healing flows,
Amidst the strife, His kindness grows.
We learn to lean on faith's embrace,
In every trial, we see His face.

A tapestry of joy and pain,
In every loss, there's so much gain.
The chronicle of life unfolds,
With every page, a truth that holds.

From darkness springs a vibrant light,
In wounded hearts, renewed in might.
Through every tear, a seed is sown,
In love and faith, we're never alone.

The Path of the Overcomer

On paths of trials, we walk with grace,
With every step, we seek His face.
In battles fierce, we find our strength,
In Christ our hope, we go the length.

The overcomers rise in faith,
With steadfast hearts, we'll not forsake.
Through storms we face, we stand our ground,
In every struggle, hope is found.

Each step a testament of love,
With guidance sent from up above.
In moments dark, our hearts ignite,
With every prayer, we choose the light.

The winding road may seem unclear,
With every step, we persevere.
In love and grace, our souls unite,
For every battle, He is our light.

Together we rise, hand in hand,
In unity, we make our stand.
The path may twist, but hearts are brave,
In faith's embrace, we are saved.

The Mosaic of the Resilient

In shards of light, we gather now,
Each piece a tale, a broken vow.
From ashes rise a hopeful song,
In unity, we all belong.

With faith the glue, we bind the light,
Through darkest hours, we find our sight.
Each color shines, a vibrant hue,
Together strong, we start anew.

From trials faced, our spirits soar,
In every crack, there's strength in more.
The mosaic forms, a living grace,
Reflecting His love, our sacred space.

With hands united, we shall stand,
In every heart, His guiding hand.
Though storms may rage, we'll never break,
In love's embrace, our lives we make.

So let us weave our stories bright,
Each thread adorned with hope's pure light.
Through every tear, each joy impart,
A masterpiece of every heart.

Heaven's Hand on Wounded Hearts

In quiet grace, the spirit mends,
With tender touch, the sorrow bends.
Each tear a prayer, we softly weave,
Together in hope, we shall believe.

Wounded hearts, like fragile glass,
In healing light, the shadows pass.
A whispered love, a soothing balm,
In Heaven's hand, we find our calm.

Through trials deep, and anguish wide,
The path is rough, but none divide.
In moments dark, we grasp His hand,
In faith and love, together stand.

Our burdens shared, our spirits lift,
In brokenness, we find the gift.
He walks with us, through waves and strife,
His light restores, it breathes us life.

So let each wound, though deep, remind,
Of Heaven's dust, our hearts entwined.
In every scar, a story told,
Of grace that shines, more pure than gold.

Unbroken Chains of Faith

In every link, a promise shared,
Through trials faced, we're gently bared.
The chains we forge in love's embrace,
United strong, we find our place.

Each broken chain shall tell a tale,
Through darkest nights, we will prevail.
In whispers soft, His presence near,
Unbroken bonds, we conquer fear.

With every prayer, we cast our nets,
In faith we stand, no regrets.
Through storms we sail, with spirits brave,
In sacred trust, our hearts we save.

Let courage rise, our voices soar,
In unity, our spirits roar.
With chains of faith, our hearts align,
Together strong, His love divine.

From shackles lost, our souls set free,
In joy we dance, in harmony.
In faith we thrive, with hope embraced,
Unbroken chains, our lives interlaced.

Illuminated by the Wounded Light

In shadows deep, we seek the glow,
From wounded hearts, the light will flow.
Each scar a beacon, guiding true,
Illuminated, we start anew.

The light of hope, through pain it shines,
In every tear, His love entwines.
Through darkest nights, our spirits gleam,
In wounded hands, we find our dream.

As morning breaks, the dawn will rise,
In every heart, a new surprise.
Together held, in love's warm light,
We dance as one, in sacred sight.

In every wound, a gift revealed,
Through faith we stand, our hearts are healed.
With grace bestowed, we shall ignite,
A world transformed, by wounded light.

So let us rise, with voices strong,
In harmony, we all belong.
With every heart, a flame inside,
Illuminated, we shall abide.

Milton Keynes UK
Ingram Content Group UK Ltd.
UKHW022224251124
451566UK00006B/112

9 789916 792216